The ever-changing Liverpool waterfront **(TK)**

I once heard Liverpool described as a city of change and challenge.

It's certainly different – just a look at the skyline from Wirral confirms the dramatic change.

But Liverpool is never a challenge, it's a natural city of character and style that is made for the camera and a good photographer's eye.

The great waterfront, St George's Hall, the houses of Toxteth, Liverpool 8 in its 60s trendy period, the cathedrals… and most of all the Liverpool people.

I have been a photographer in Liverpool for over 40 years and I have always worked with a talented team of photographers at the Daily Post & Echo.

They never fail to capture exciting pictures of the city in all seasons and the top awards won by the photographic team outnumber those of any other regional newspaper.

For Liverpool Now we have selected some of our very best Daily Post & Echo images – I hope you enjoy them.

– Stephen Shakeshaft, Picture Editor, Liverpool Daily Post & Echo

A firework display at the Metropolitan Cathedral of Christ The King (EB)

Top National Museums Liverpool's 1909 Burnell traction engine out for a spin past Waterloo Dock, in preparation for the annual Woodvale Rally **(AT)**
Above Picnic in the gardens at St George's Hall **(SS)**

Above More than just neighbours – the terraces of Toxteth are a family affair **(EB)**

Shades
of Autumn

By Colin Lane

Colin joined the Liverpool Daily Post & Echo
in 1995. He has been working as a staff
photographer on Merseyside for 18 years,
starting at Mercury Press agency in 1989.
Influenced by his uncle John, a keen amateur
photographer, Colin started taking pictures at
the age of 12. Keen to pursue a career as a
sports photographer, Colin went from taking
pictures of local teams Liverpool and Everton
to international matches and Wembley finals
in just a couple of years. Since then he has
covered many finals including th FA Cup,
Milk Cup, UEFA and Champions League.
Colin says: **"Liverpool is a unique city for
sport, not just football but boxing, racing,
athletics and much more. It is a strong news
city with passionate people – the New York
of Europe!**

 **"My most memorable assignment with
the Post & Echo was when I was sent to
New York, USA, with two prize winners who
were representing the city for a parade in
central park to launch the opening of
Disney's Animal Kingdom. They were part of
a dance routine performed by several
hundred children from around the world,
in which they made the shapes of animals.
"I was stationed on a crane hundreds of feet
up (at eye-level with the New York skyline!)
to shoot down on the parade – what a view.
"Oh and how can I forget a certain
Champions League match in Istanbul –
Liverpool v AC Milan. Great drama, amazing
city and fantastic pictures, some of which
brought me the highest honour of my career
when I was named The British Picture Editors
Getty Images Regional Photographer of the
Year winner in 2006."**

I was sent to take a straightforward interior shot of The Quarter restaurant/café bar on Faulkner Street in the city, for an eating-out guide. When I walked in, to my delight, there was a stream of warm sunlight pouring in. This picture, which I call Shades of Autumn, has a real Parisian feel to it. It has proved popular with friends, family and colleagues – it is now on the walls of quite a few Merseyside homes! Some people have compared this picture, with its lightened colours, to the work of American artist Edward Hopper! The success of the picture continued when it won a Special Award in the UK Picture Editors Awards in 2004, when I was named The Getty Images Regional Photographer Of The Year. My prize was presented by Prime Minister Tony Blair at the Guild Hall in London

Architecture at the Pier Head (SS)

Top   Rotten night out – Sex Pistols fans take over The Cavern **(EB)**

Above Anti-Iraq war protestors make their voices heard outside Liverpool Town Hall **(EB)**

A tranquil summer scene… the Pavillion at Abercromby Square Gardens, near Oxford Street, in the heart of the University of Liverpool campus (AT)

3

LIVERPOOL NOW

Top Dummy run: The Southport Air Show is rained off **(EB)**
Above Toxteth's 'Bread' Streets from the air **(EB)**

Tall ship The Phoenix arrives on the River Mersey passing the Liver Buildings for the start of the Mersey River Festival **(AT)**

Top Footballers and flowers in Stanley Park, Anfield **(EB)**
Above Evidence of Liverpool's maritime heritage **(HD)**

Blinking heck! A spectacular wall of water forms a screen for a Sefton Park light show **(EB)**

A hundred years, a thousand stories

By Martin Birchall

Martin has been a photographer with the Daily Post & Echo for 17 years.
He came to Merseyside from the Bolton Evening News and has contributed to various national papers and magazines.
Martin's lifetime ambition is to record events for others to enjoy and believes that every day

Liverpool offers great picture opportunities with its people, love of life and fantastic architecture. Martin was delighted to be sent to cover the Commonwealth Games Finals for the Post & Echo. Another of his most memorable photographic assignments was covering the Battle Of the Atlantic fleet celebrations.

He says: **"I flew for over four hours in a Sea King helicopter, spending most of the time strapped to the outside of the helicopter over the top of the Royal Yacht Britannia in gale force winds. The final picture captured waves crashing over the bow – with the helicopter pilot keeping me steady over the top of the yacht."**

Patrick in his earlier days

A portrait of a man that will not be forgotten in years to come – Patrick Lunt, the oldest carter in Liverpool. More than one hundred years ago the first cries were heard from a little boy who would ride through depressions, wars and parades to become Liverpool's oldest carter. This portrait shows a man full of expression and character, a true legend who has seen a lot of life and a lot of changes. Patrick began work in 1920, pulling a handcart from house to house for a local bakery after leaving St Anthony's Parish School on Scotland Road, Liverpool, at the age of 14. As a young man he worked at George Davies and Son, a haulage firm with its main HQ on Chapel Street. Working in short pants, his first wage was 50p a week. In this portrait, taken at the ripe old age of 100, Patrick's enthusiasm for life shines in his face and his expression, with his last remaining tooth, gives me inspiration

An aerial shot of the of Liverpool's Pier Head, showing the Liver Building, the Cunard Building and the Port of Liverpool Building, which makes it one of the world's most impressive and talked about waterfronts (JR)

A sunny day under an arch of fruit trees at Croxteth Country Park (EB)

Top   Olympic medallist Steve Parry after the annual Boxing Day swim at Albert Dock **(EB)**
Above Santa Dashers phone home after the charity run **(EB)**

Top Traditional butcher's skills are still in practice on Scotland Road **(EB)**
Above Netherton youngsters put some bounce into their day **(EB)**

Top Fountain of youth – Williamson Square photographed from the Radio City tower **(EB)**
Above Goal! Beach football at New Brighton **(EB)**

Transported to Another Place

By Eddie Barford

For the past 40 years, Eddie Barford has been observing his home city through the lens of a Liverpool Daily Post & Echo camera.
He says: "Most of what I have seen I have liked. From the openness of the people – sometimes in the face of great adversity – to the wit of a chance remark that can leave you chuckling all day."
Eddie's camera has taken him on assignments from the private office of the heir to the throne in Kensington Palace to the Golan Heights for a feature on the Holy Land and, of course, to every corner of Merseyside.
Eddie says: "Picture assignments that stick in my mind include the headless ghost of Rufford Hall (sorry boss, no pic!), the terminally ill woman who married her sweetheart in a hospital room and the cold glint in the eye of a child murderer in an image snatched through the window of a prison van.
"I am proud to be part of a tradition of photographers who have recorded the images that reflect our great city's history and its people; pictures that capture a moment in time. A newspaper photographer has to be detached but that is just about impossible when working in this city, where our papers are part of the family."

Another Place, another sunny day in Crosby

Top A statue of Minerva looks over the city from Liverpool Town Hall (JR)
Above Imagine… John Lennon's statue looks down Mathew Street (AT)

And they're off! Fallen National Jockeys watch the action at Aintree **(EB)**

Top Victorian charm – the ornate Empress pub nestles next to Toxteth's Welsh Streets.
The pub featured on Ringo Starr's solo album Sentimental Journey **(EB)**

Above Almost like a stage, the leading lady in the floodlight is the Royal Liver Building **(TO)**

The Duke of Wellington statue looks down on the city, dwarfing St George's Hall. I was asked to take pictures of the statue's restoration and was lucky to go up in a large cherry-picker alongside the statue. From here I was able to capture this unique Wellington's eye view **(CL)**

Eric Wheeler the last of the Liverpool carters, is loyal to horse power. He drives a horse-drawn bus, his son drives a horse-drawn cab and Eric delivers the goods around Kirkdale and Everton with his horse and cart. The kids still come out to watch him… who needs the internet?!

Tradition
kept alive

By Stephen Shakeshaft

Stephen Shakeshaft is the picture editor for the Daily Post & Echo.

He has been a photographer in Liverpool for 43 years and his photographs have been published world-wide. Stephen's picture of Archbishop Derek Worlock and Bishop David Sheppard was on exhibition at the National Portrait Gallery as a picture of the century. He was Royal Photographer of the Year in 1988 and he has won over 40 awards for photography.

Two of Stephen's exhibitions at the Museum of Liverpool Life and Liverpool Conservation Centre attracted over 100,000 people. Soccer Shots was a showcase of Merseyside soccer heroes and Shooting Stars showed celebrities and politicians behind the scenes. Stephen has won two British Picture Editor Awards for Arts with his photographs of Ken Dodd.

A tot calls the shots at Liverpool Town Hall (EB)

A beautiful summer's day at Haskayne (**EB**)

Seasons make such a difference to photographers. Here the late summer sun makes Sefton Park look particularly special (TK)

Top   Sir Bob Scott and Mike Storey celebrate Liverpool's Capital Of Culture win **(EB)**
Above A unique view of Liverpool and Wirral from the Mersey Ferry **(EB)**

This shot of the Liverpool skyline in the late afternoon mist was taken in December 2005. It captured the changing face of the city, with its buildings, cranes and the famous Liver Birds in the distance. The city was covered with an unusual eerie mist and knowing the Everton area with its panoramic views, and the assistance of a fabulous sunset silhouetting the city all helped me to capture this unusual shot

Changing city in the mist

By Andrew Teebay

Andrew Teebay has worked at the Daily Post & Echo for 12 years.
He joined the Liverpool team from sister papers The Southport Visiter, Crosby Herald and Bootle Times.
Andrew has had a keen interest in photography since childhood, owning his first camera from the age of 15, a Pentax ME Super!.
Andrew says: **"As a former Echo paper boy, I used to flick through the papers and look at the great pictures inside, especially the football. This inspired me to become a photographer.**

"Liverpool is a vibrant and amazing city to photograph and work in, with its historic buildings, cathedrals, music, waterfront, sport, humour and investment for the 2008 European Capital of Culture.

"The Daily Post & Echo photographers have always had a great reputation, and it's a privilege to work alongside a great team."
Andrew's most memorable photographic assignment for the Post & Echo was covering the recent takeover of Liverpool Football Club by Hicks and Gillett, making headlines around the world.

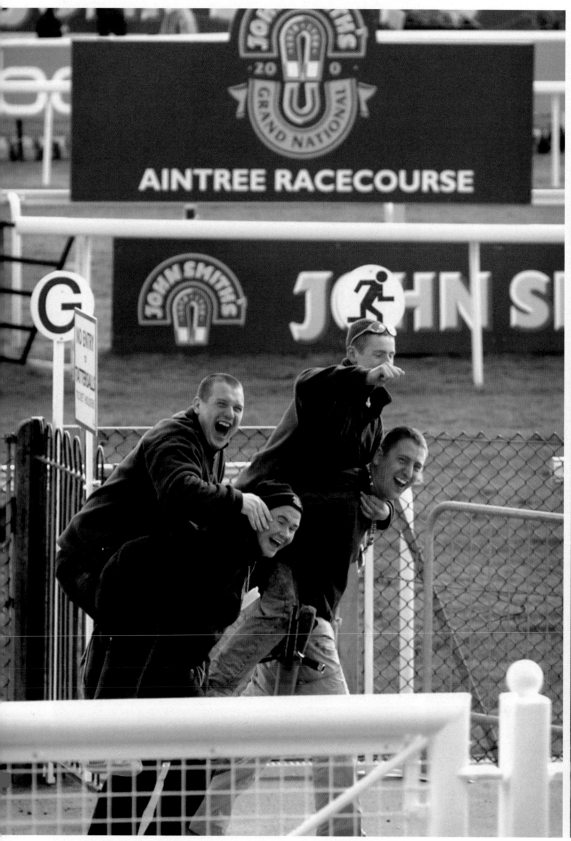

Horse play at Aintree (EB)

The leaving of Liverpool – A clipper race crew member bids farewell to his girlfriend at the Albert Dock **(EB)**

Top No kidding – celebrating the Year of the Goat in Chinatown **(EB)**
Above Powerboat racing on the Mersey – a new event in Liverpool's sporting calendar **(TK)**

Liverpool's Queen Square bathed in sunshine and shadows **(EB)**

New light on old windows

By Howard Davies

Howard Davies joined the Post & Echo
35 years ago, straight from school.
He began taking pictures when he
was very young, sharing his father's interest in
photography and borrowing his camera.
Howard enjoys working in Liverpool,
as **"it is a very news active city, with a rich
cultural history"**.
If he could take pictures at any event in
history, Howard would love to have been at
the tickertape parade for the Apollo II
astronauts on Broadway in New York in 1969,
after their return from the moon.
Howard's most memorable photographic
assignment for the Post and Echo wasn't
quite as glamourous…
He says: **"I was once the only photographer
on a visit by Prince Charles to a TA training
camp on the Isle of Man and was charged
by the regimental mascot, a goat!"**

Although a much-photographed building, this shot caught the
dramatic floodlighting on Liverpool Town Hall. I took this shot
at half past midnight

A rear view of Doddy… Who else?! (SS)

Top   Liverpool FC fans watch their heroes on the giant Clayton Square screen **(EB)**
Above Lads take a view over a city centre fountain **(EB)**

48

Left Springtime in Sefton Park (SS)
Right Ancient and modern – a gaslight outside the Unity Building (SS)

Port Sunlight Lyceum band members promote the Playhouse **(EB)**

Formby point from the air, showing the beauty of the Merseyside coastline. I had this photo as a screensaver on my laptop during the visit of the US Secretary of State Condoleezza Rice to Liverpool. I was sending some pictures back to the office when one of the American Embassy security officials came over to ask: "Was that beach in Australia?" I took great pleasure telling him it was just 30 miles up the road! **(CL)**

Peter Crouch celebrates in front of the Kop as the Reds score against West Ham (MB)

Top   Sunrise over the city at the start of New Year 2007. The Anglican cathedral dominates the skyline way above the crane towers **(MB)**
Above Liverpool's Albert Dock with its railway buffers – a reminder of the days when it was a working dock **(HD)**

Liver, but not as we know it

By Tracey O'Neill

Tracey O'Neill has been working for the Post & Echo for 16 years.
Before joining the Liverpool team Tracey worked at Manchester-based press agency Quay Photographic where she was involved in all types of press work from news, features, sport and magazines to studio glamour and table-top product shots.
Says Tracey: "My father was a photographic manager of three national newspapers, so newspapers and photography had always been a part of my life. Still now the smell of dev in a darkroom will take me back to greeting my father in the morning when he came in from his night shift. It was no surprise to anybody when I announced what I was planning on doing with my life. One of the earlier pictures of me is when I was three, photographing my friends."
Tracey is proud to work in Liverpool:
"Being a photographer you are a chronicler of today for tomorrow, capturing images of the city, surroundings and of course its people in every situation possible. You are privileged to be accepted into people's lives at their most memorable times, whether in happiness or extreme sadness. I am always surprised by the hearts and generosity of the people of Liverpool, a truly unique city."
Tracey's most memorable assignment for the Post & Echo was flying over Wales in a Hawk jet from RAF Valley: "The paper had received complaints about noise pollution from the jets, so a reporter and I were sent there to have a look around. Our flight lasted an hour and was truly spectacular, something I shall never forget. I'm sure the pilot wont forget it in a hurry either – after 10 minutes I became extremely ill…"

I'm sure most photographers have stacks of images of the Liver Birds. This image appeals to me because its one of the few times the building has looked so abstract. The image is not manipulated, simply reflected in the Beetham Plaza windows

The sky was so moody, dark and angry, perfect for black and white photography. Reflections of the cool, crisp yachts add interest in the foreground and the Anglican cathedral stands proud and majestic, looking on **(TO)**

Top   Paddling with the wind turbines in New Brighton **(EB)**
Above One of Liverpool's oldest and most popular watering holes "Ye Cracke" **(EB)**

Still the perfect place to sunbathe! **(EB)**

Humour in its candid form – many times a picture has presented itself without the subject realising the funny side **(SS)**

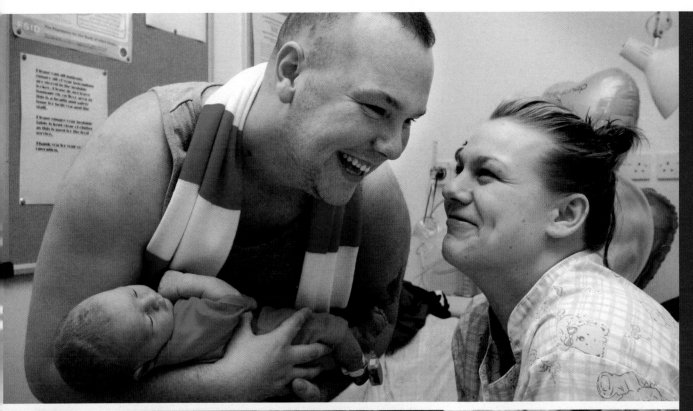

Top Just champion: Mad keen Liverpool fan Kevin Tremarco with baby Joel Anthony and mum Claire Mason **(EB)**

Above Everton take on Liverpool and Blues manager David Moyes celebrates Andy Johnson's goal – Everton's third during the derby game **(MB)**

A youngster finds a quiet place to weave her magic in Liverpool Museum **(EB)**

Top Three wise men make a stark and moving picture against the Liverpool skyline
as they gather for the Christmas celebrations at Everton Heights **(EB)**

Above This cat seems to have grabbed the best seat for the Mathew Street Festival **(EB)**

"The Gash" at Williamson Tunnels – the entrance to the underground banqueting hall dug by the workers of the Mole Of Edge Hill (EB)

Top The Wheeler family have been involved with horses in the city for over 80 years and, keeping tradition, the Landau pulled by Paddy the horse operates from William Brown Street **(MB)**

Above The end of the Clipper Race as the boats sail past the Albert Dock **(TK)**

As a photographer you find yourself looking for that different photograph. By shooting through the circular shape, I was not constricted to a square or rectangular picture window. I wanted to illustrate new growth in the city combining artwork and construction **(TO)**

Top A break for the taxi at the Albert Dock **(SS)**
Above Reflections on a summer's day in Mathew Street **(EB)**

Top   Heading home for a good cuppa on a chilly winter's day in Hightown **(EB)**
Above Rod Codman and Mr Punch **(SS)**

A classic case of right place at the right time! I was driving back to the office along the dock road and I could see the Yakolevs aerial display team flying in the distance during the Mersey River Festival celebrations. With the dark sky approaching I drove up to The Strand and timed it just right with two frames as the display team flew over the Liver Birds. This picture won the Trinity Mirror Best Regional Daily Picture of the Year award in 2005 **(CL)**

Still one of the great attractions for visitors – the ferry ride across the Mersey (TK)

This land's the place I love

By Tony Kenwright

"I can't bring myself to say it, but Shankly managed Liverpool and The Beatles had only just split up when I became a photographer."
As a youngster, Tony Kenwright had his heart set on being a photographer, using his dad's dark room ("a blacked-out bathroom") to print his own pictures.

Tony worked at a bank for 15 months when he left school, a job he hated and which makes him appreciate his job at the Daily Post & Echo even more.

Tony has brought us pictures from many landmark events over the years.

"I remember hundreds of them. Some, like Hillsborough, for all the wrong reasons," says Tony. "Covering Liverpool in the days of Paisley/Fagan and Dalglish was tremendous. Photographing Bob Dylan in Newcastle in 1984 was memorable too. Perhaps for the most memorable, I'd better say the school play in 1982 where I met my wife!"

If he could photograph any event, past or present, Tony would choose the golden days of Hollywood.

"Imagine photographing Humphrey Bogart or Ingrid Bergman on the set of Casablanca, or Fay Wray in King Kong's grasp," he says. "Ultimately though, I'd love a one to one with Elvis…"

DAFFODIL

The Palm House at Sefton Park (SS)

Youngsters cool off in the Leeds/Liverpool canal at Vauxhall (EB)

Top Dog roses at the Pier Head **(SS)**

Above Dense fog covered the city and I went to the top floor at the Post & Echo offices and to my amazement the only building visible was the Anglican Cathedral as it towered above the fog in the late afternoon November sunset. The picture reminds me of the photographs from the Blitz in London when St Paul's cathedral towered above the smoke after the air raids **(CL)**

Top Gasps of delight as the Merchant Taylors girls get their A Level results **(EB)**
Above A wedding day kiss for these American visitors, married at the gates of Strawberry Field **(EB)**

Any city takes on a different feel at night. Dusk is a magical time leaving enough light to capture the form of the clouds. You are able to pick up the reflections and colours of the boats and street lamps (TO)

The good old dock road again. I was driving back to the office one summer's evening in heavy monsoon-style rain when, in the distance, a shaft of sunlight opened up across Wirral onto the Pier Head. It cast an incredible Mars-like colour on the buildings with the storm clouds and sky behind (CL)

A dad brings his young child to see Cunard liner The Caronia **(EB)**

Fireworks over the Walker Art Gallery to celebrate Liverpool's 800th birthday (TK)

Top A young fisherman casts his line out at Sefton Park lake **(EB)**
Above The Tranmere Rovers girls… and their tea stall **(SS)**

Scotland Road drinkers enjoy some glamorous company **(EB)**

Top Dream Day: The first civil partnership ceremony takes place in Liverpool Town Hall **(EB)**
Above The Capital of Culture 'Celebrating City Life' flag, under Liverpool's famous landmark the Liver Building **(JR)**

Sailing into
the sunset

By Jason Roberts

Jason has worked at the Liverpool Daily Post
& Echo as a staff photographer for about five
years, joining the Liverpool team from the
Chester Chronicle, where he was employed
as a staff photographer for two years.
Prior to that he worked as a freelance at
photographic agency Creative Photography
from 1986 until 2000.
Jason got his first camera when he was just
five years old, a present from his father who
was a keen amateur photographer.
Says Jason: "I just had a passion for taking
pictures and I thought, what a way to make
a living!"
"I like working in Liverpool because it is a
great news city as well as having top
football teams, (well, one – Liverpool FC!).
It also has the best waterfront in the world
bar none and a great creative arts and
entertainment scene."
If he could photograph anything, past or
present, Jason's dream assignment would have
been covering the 1966 World Cup final.
A big football fan, Jason was delighted when
the Post & Echo sent him to Turin to cover
the Juventus v Liverpool game in the quarter
finals of the Champions League 2005.

These canoeists, dwarfed by the magnificence of the Albert
Dock at dusk, have an unrivalled view

Stephanie Davies from Liverpool Comedy Trust with pupils from Bedford Primary School, Bootle, destressing before SAT tests (MB)

Marilyn Monroe lookalike Melita Morgan struts her stuff at Albert Dock **(EB)**

The Palm House at Sefton Park (SS)

Top Freddie Starr has a laugh with hairdresser Herbert during his Mother's Day offer for Echo mums at his salon and empire (MB)
Above The grand St George's Hall lit up during the Brouhaha Festival in the city (CL)

The sun sets and the day comes to an end over the city (JR)

The statue of the Rt Hon Sir Arthur Bower Forwood Baronet looks down on passing schoolchildren in St John's Gardens **(AT)**

So that's a rap. A grandad and his young charge leave Rice Lane Farm, Walton, after enjoying an urban music festival **(EB)**